WHO'S THAT BOY

Poetry Collection

By

Deluke Muwanigwa

COPYRIGHT © 2021 WHO'S THAT BOY
By Deluke Muwanigwa

ISBN:
Hardbound- 978-621-8261-43-3
Softbound- 978-621-8261-42-6
Mobile/Kindle- 978-621-8261-41-9

Published by Poetry Planet Book Publishing House
Edited by Marie Ezekiel
Designed by Tess Ritumalta
Cover photo by Deluke Muwanigwa

Some photos used are taken on Pinterest and may contain their copyrights

DEDICATION

I would like to dedicate this collection of poetry to Barbara, my wife, and my two grown-up kids, Dananayi and Mudiwa Nathasia. They understood the lonely moments I spent on my own trying to conjure up images and metaphors. They read my drafts and commented and it is from their comments I derived courage to share my poetry with the world.

ACKNOWLEDGEMENTS

I want to acknowledge the following people who in one way or another made these works possible.

My wife Barbara Muwanigwa. My Barbie Doll. I took a lot of her "me time" to write these poems.

My son, Dananayi, and my daughter, Nathasia Mudiwa. They read and said, "Wow, can you write another!".

Poetry Planet Publishing House for editing and doing most of the hard work to produce these works.

My poet friends, Robert Murray Smith of Australia, M Asim Nehal of India, Poetess Varsha Madhulika who read and told me it was rubbish when it was, well, rubbish.

Madam Geeta Radhakrishna Menon of India.

-My countryman Phillip Nine Mafunga.

There are many other poets from all over the world who held my poetic hands knowingly or unknowingly. To all of them, it's kudos from me.

Deluke Muwanigwa

PREFACE

I have so many things to say. I have had so many things to say. Desires, regrets, ideas, and, sometimes, just saying stuff for the sake of saying stuff. I try to speak, but no one listens. I try to write, but no one reads. No one!

I am fortunate that I have found another way to express myself. Poetry! With poetry, I can express myself in a few lines. My fears, my wants, my desires, and fantasies in a few lines. Fantastic! This book, which I hope readers will enjoy, is hopefully the first of many. As long as I live I will always have an opinion and I enjoy expressing myself in poetry.

Some people who thought they had me all figured out will be, in some cases, horribly surprised, and in other cases, pleasantly surprised. I ask that the reader keeps an open mind and come with me on my debut poetry journey. Whatever be your final impression I want you to know I love you too. Enjoy!

Deluke Muwanigwa, C. 2021.

TABLE OF CONTENTS

Copyright 2

Dedication 3

Acknowledgements 4

Preface 5

I Love My Attitude Problem 12

Our Class 14

Poetic Jungle 15

Nativity 17

Rhythm Confessions 18

Still A Man 20

Don't Let 22

Masks And Fears 23

Burden Of Being Me 25

Error Message In Mirror? 26

I Don't Understand 28

Just The Way You Are 29

Good Tidings 30

What If What If 31

Walking In A Blind World 32

The Reach Man 34

Love Me Silly 36

The Demon's Sermon..37

Being Good Is Not Always Good 38

A Perfect Person 40

Ism Isn't..41

Be Sure 43

Never Say It, Show It..44

Life Is Too Short 45

My Love Never Takes A Day Off..47

Life And Death..48

My Friend 50

You, Me, Maybe 52

Who's That Girl?..53

Keep Your Opinion As Open As The Gates Of Heaven..55

Rhyming Is Nine Tenth The Flow..56

S.A.W.S..59

Unknown Time To An Unknown Destination.................60

The Last Day 61

Street Poetry....Devil In The Dark..62

Far Far Away..63

Hallelujah 65

Poemyelitis?..66

Life Is.... 67

Wait And See 69

Nature Doesn't Care 71

Nature Never Fails 73

Surprise Surprise 74

Street Poetry...Replacing Door Glass 75

In Love With You 77

Making Sense Of The Senseless 78

Comfort Zones 80

Would You...If I Gave You My Heart? 81

Time Will Tell 82

This Thing Called Kissing 83

The Emotion Of A Real Man 84

I Promise 85

Never Again 86

I Wrote A Ballad 87

When You Said Yes! Yes! Yes! 88

I Want It 89

I Shall, I Will 90

They Kneel To Pray 91

Naked Lies 92

"Read The Cliché" 93

My Brain Tells Me This, My Heart That, My Soul The
Arbiter 94

Sound Love..96

Words...98

Retreat Treaty 99

Soul Searching......................................101

We Trip Whichever Way 103

Some...104

Having Fun, Having Pun 105

Waking Up To The Unknown 107

I'm Staying..108

When I Part My Lips To Talk To You.............110

Acrostic Caustic Poem.............................112

Re-Write...113

When I.....I...114

Blessings..115

In My Life..116

Society Expects.....................................118

So Deep, For Keeps 119

Cross..120

My Word 121

Just Love?...123

A Rebel With A Cause Rebelling For No Reason 124

Back To My Roots...................................125

Because I Love You.................................127

The Longest Minute In The World 128

Love Timetable..129

Human Relationships May Be Like That......................130

That's Me 131

Write It Down..132

Sometimes In Anger There Is Truth 133

May Little Ones Warm Your Heart.............................135

I Can't Keep Calm Because You Excite Me 136

I Go Through The Rusty Shelves Of My Life 137

Sometimes I Am Up, Sometimes I Am Down.............139

The Mind 140

Bridge To Riversdale Farm 141

About The Author 142

I LOVE MY ATTITUDE PROBLEM

I love my attitude problem
Gets people irritated and resentful
Most of the time the issue is with them

Most of the time the issue is with them
They lack a keen sense of humour
Most of the time I don't give a damn

I love my attitude problem
Gives me freedom for quick wit
Laughing at situations without blame

Most of the time the issue is with them
Carrying stereotypes and prejudices
In a way, I provoke a reaction good or bad all the
same

I love my attitude problem
Gives me freedom to see poetic situations others
won't
I run along with any poetry program

There is a serious problem with my fame
Sometimes my attitude gets me in trouble but not
out

I love my attitude problem
Most of the time the issue is with them.

OUR CLASS

In my poetry ideals
Sometimes I have strange ideas
Ideas like sand in an hourglass
Radical in their own unique class
Isn't that how it should be?
For each to be free
To express
Timeless
An Iota
It
Fits
In stricture
The structure
Of an hourglass
Allows ideas to pass
The good, the bad, and the ugly
To fit in the annals of time smugly
Two thousand years ago I know
Idea of a phone was a no no
Now all over your face
A new modern phase
Let ideas cross hole
Let them flow
In the jar
Into
Hourglass
Of our class

POETIC JUNGLE

This year I got lost in a jungle
A jungle of vases and roses
And verses and proses
There, the trees having sonnets for bark
Branches of thyme waving in time with crime
Villanelle a villain in the village foliage
The phantom in Pantoum
Is it Kharthoum where the tomb in the pyramid
gets rapid?
Intrepid
Trapping vowels and consonants
And vows of voyages of discovery by astronauts.
Looking for the summer solstice
My soul reciting without notice
"A midsummer night's dream"
A bald man shaking a spear
But I had no fear
The poetry jungle exciting
Enticing

I met many crazies like me
A spectacle to see
Some lost in frost
Not sure which river to cross
Many dead on arrival

An unnecessary rival
Ain't sure I will escape
My castle far from the Cape
The Cape of Good Hope
For life there's scope
A home away from home
Empire of Rome in prose

Viaducts of emotion
Walls of intonation
Rivers of rhyme
Solemn like the Rhine
No dissonance
More assonance
Reasonableness
Resonance
Harmony
No harm on me
My abode humble
My poetry jungle

NATIVITY

She was inexperienced
Quite young
He, wised up
Gone there, done that
She at his mercy
Sacrificial lass

Fate had it
Union blessed
Pioneers of man
In the garden
The activity
Nativity

Man loves woman
Woman loves man
Man looks after Earth
Earth looks after Man
Earth dying
Man crying

RHYTHM CONFESSIONS

I will redeem my poetry
My Rhythm Confessions
I will try not to rhyme
I will cry in abject pain
I am so used to couplets
I am so abused by poetic sound

Makes me sick
Takes me time to heal
Like the heart of a jilted lover
Like a part of my poetry infected
Bad is the day self-expression dies
Sad is the way people judge you
As if judgement day isn't coming
At least I should be free a bird in a tree till the day

I am choking
I am smoking in my brain
A clutch on a steep slope
As such labouring
Not to rhyme
Hot is my soul
I ask my spirit
Task my telepathy
It says it's busy

It pays to be patient

"Please try again later"
"The number you dialed is not available"

I wait in the morning
I wait in the afternoon
I wait at night
I am still waiting
I am, till eternity
To redeem myself
My rhythm Confessions

STILL A MAN

Whatever he did was outsized
Wherever he went ostracized
Ego a soaring eagle
Bragging through a bugle
A man of excesses

Had castles in the air
with golden stairs
Real estate in every state
Dealmaker his fate
Proof wrapped in excuses

A bone to chew
A phone call to screw
A victim
A victory
Losing he obsesses

He is still a man
A man
He tries
He cries
Place face in space with his failures and successes.

He is a man
Still a man.
A man.

DON'T LET

Don't let
Anyone bring you down
And treat you like a clown

Don't let
Any one stop you
And treat you like a fool

Don't let
Anyone make you doubt your dream
And treat you like you are short of steam

Don't let
Any one's opinion be your ultimate guide
And treat you like you have no pride

"Life is too short"
Your retort!
Even as they deport.

MASKS AND FEARS

23

Masquerading
Parading
Money
With honeys
Ignoring monsoon
Coming soon
The pestilence
The persistence

Triolette of hoity toity
Haute hippie faulty
Three musketeers
Free master beerers
Breathing free
The pollen from tree
Contaminated
Concatenated

Musketeers
Masks and tears
Be wise
Sanitize
End of day
Nothing to say
Caskets and tears
Masks and fears

BURDEN OF BEING ME

My mother tried and cried
To mould me into a good child
I thank my mum for the effort

My father, tempted, attempted
To understand why I was wild
Bordered on abuse his effrontery

Society double struggled
To make my manners mild
by law and order enforcement

God knows I fight day and night
Apply my mind to be good and kind
I arrive at the same rhetorical retrospective what
fors

This is me
Whatever you think and believe, the being you see
is me
The burden of being me

ERROR MESSAGE IN MIRROR?

These days I look in the mirror
I see a new era
Something is wrong
My feeling strong
I don't see a reflection of myself
Is it a gnome or is it an elf?
This effigy
This refugee
An alien visitor
An avatar
Ecdysis?
Metamorphosis?
Whatever it is
I don't like this

Is it old age?
At the stage?
Hair grey
Temper frayed
Impatient
A patient
On life support pills
Depressing thrills
I fear lasses
Wear glasses

My eye
Am I?
Seeing me in the mirror?
Error message in the mirror?

I DON'T UNDERSTAND

I don't understand why you don't understand
We have been given a once in a lifetime
opportunity to live
Billions of spermatozoon would have wanted a
chance

You triumphed thrived survived and lived

We have been given a once in a lifetime
opportunity to live
Why then do you say this place is not your home?
You triumphed thrived survived and lived
Are you not better placed to live, love and
bequeath the future?

Why then do you say this place is not your home?
Billions of spermatozoon would have wanted a
chance
Are you not better placed to live love and bequeath
the future?
I don't understand why you don't understand.

JUST THE WAY YOU ARE

You want perfection from me
Do a list let me see
Of what a flawless me would be
Carte blanche, do it be free

Perhaps a little taller?
My drive a little smaller?
The way I talk?
Perhaps even the way I walk?

Go deep
Nothing skip
My complexion?
A complication?

When you are done comparing
When are done conferring
Know that I've gone near and far
I love you just the way you are

Psychologically pleasing
Physiologically teasing
My one and only baby mama
I love you just the way you are

GOOD TIDINGS

I see visions of a good year coming
And that counts for something
Otherwise it's been mounds of bad news
A year of bad issues

The world at crossroads
As if we crossed the Lord
Prayers bouncing off deaf ears
Faces drenched in forlorn tears

Sure as the sun rises to set
We expect things to let
We expect no longer to be mournful
We remain hopeful

Where there's life there's hope
So our brows we mope
And look forward to a better life
Good tidings to all mankind

WHAT IF WHAT IF

What if what if is no longer just a wishful question?
When what if is no longer what if but what is?
Will you be counted among other pioneers?
Ready to serve your people and all mankind

When what if is no longer what if but what is
Would our assumptions have been redone to a
new reality?
Ready to serve your people and all mankind
Will we be freed of traditional beliefs that drag us
down?

Would our assumptions have been redone to a
new reality?
Will you be counted among other pioneers?
Will we be freed of traditional beliefs that drag us
down?
What if what if is no longer just a wishful question?

WALKING IN A BLIND WORLD

32

Walking in a blind world
People with eyes who can't see
Their range limited by assumptions
Multimedia slavery
Flashing words and pictures
Doctored reality
A comfort zone
Fiction
Friction

Is it true then reality can be made?
Like the reality of the sun
That it rises in the east
We could have called it west
The sun will still rise
Manufactured consent
A convenient way to live
Easy to accept
The truth to except

Stubborn like the sun
The truth
Send a Parker Probe
Get up real close
It's expensive
It's not easy
The luminosity opens our eyes for posterity
Regrettably, we believe someone's weird word
Walking in a blind world

THE REACH MAN

Familiarity with riches tempts
With the ability you attempt
Everything has a price
Everyone bought with rice
Your loot playing the lute
The Pied Piper you dilute
Your perspective de facto reality
Corrupted system confers legality
You are the rich man
The reach man

The reach man
The rich man
Is it then that you know all there is to know?
Indigenous knowledge not at all?
Your point of view
Makes everyone your fool
Dissenters refrain
Suppressed without restraint

Rich man
Reach man
Preach man
Teach man
From your power
From your tower
The rich man
Alas, is the reach man

LOVE ME SILLY

You are my filly
Truly fully
Really really
Love me fully

Wishes be horses
I'd sing my voice till it hoarses
No pauses
Same clauses

You are my filly
Truly fully
Really really
Love me fully

Love me fully
Love me truly fully
Love me really truly
Love me silly.

THE DEMON'S SERMON

My oh my
What style
Such oratory skills
Giving thrills
Deceit buried in sweetness
Ringfenced with strictness

Before you know
Deep your fall
In a trance.
You prance and dance
You have arrived
Reality deprived

The demon's sermon
Demon's sermon
Afflictive
Addictive
The sermon
The demon

BEING GOOD IS NOT ALWAYS GOOD

Being good is not always good
Some people take it as a sign of weakness
Instead of reciprocating treat you rude.

Instead of reciprocating treat you rude
As if they have a right and you don't
Spoiling your good mood.

Being good is not always good
Meekness is taken as a weakness
And yet all we all want is to be understood.

Instead of reciprocating treat you rude
Patronizing pettiness personified
Even the language used is crude

Being good is not always good
You become someone everyone finds loathsome
The fall guy in the neighborhood

So it pays to stand your ground and demand an
equal share of the food
Otherwise, they take advantage of you.
Instead of reciprocating treat you rude
Being good is not always good.

A PERFECT PERSON

A perfect person
Is not perfect per se
It's a person suffering disaffection
Seeking solace in pseudo affection

Isn't a perfect person boring?
Making an issue of snoring?
Always point-scoring?
And scorn pouring?

We need less of, not more
So we can get in the door.
Of the perfect person
Putting our normal face on

ISM ISN'T

Communism is not humanism
Capitalism is not a cataclysm
Racism is not apartheid
Fascism is not skinheads

They are isms
Ideas in prisms
People in prison
For no good reason.

Free your mind
For humankind
In the fallacies
Find balances

I know what I want
Despite the strident rant
I know what I like
I want a good life

When the firebrand stands at the podium
Whips up emotion like an isotope of Uranium
Sodium
Remember history
Hysteria is not a mystery

Ism isn't
It isn't it
It isn't pleasing
Ism isn't

BE SURE

Here we are alone
At home
Go ahead undress
But there are issues to address
This dress you want to impress
What is the address
from which you got it?
Before I stress what gives me stress
and you use the hot iron to press the dress to
express yourself
Is this want you want?
because to reverse we can't
Don't be demure
Be sure

NEVER SAY IT, SHOW IT

Never say it
Be fair
Show it

Show it
Words are hot air
Do every bit

Never say it
I have been hurt before
There on the street

Show it
That I am worthy
Be discrete

Never say it
It's been said before
By every twit

Otherwise, forget it
You're just the same
Never say it
Show it.

LIFE IS TOO SHORT

45

What good is wearing a bad mood?
When the program and the problem are
understood
The probability of the morbidity and your humility
Mutually exclusive even with antitussives
Don't worry be happy don't hurry to feel crappy
Be still in your house of stone where you were born
The time to atone will come, your life don't abort
Because life is too short

Homie, wear your mask
Your new daily task
Wash those hands
Stay in your bands
Don't panic
Don't be manic
Your life don't ignore
Because life is too short.

Not being liked is alike like being liked.
It's nice to be liked but nicer to be alive
We stand arms akimbo like true Zimbos
Life in limbo but still nimble
Having fun under the sun, we pun
Laughing, joking, poking, smoking
We drink, we snort
Alas, life is too short

MY LOVE NEVER TAKES A DAY OFF

I sense the doubt in you
In love, it's nothing new
The battle of the sexes
So many calling each other exes

I know your heart is precious
You play your cards cautious
Close to your chest, you must
You need to give me your trust

I am rock steady in love
To give lots of it and some
Solid like the Rock of Gibraltar
Ready for the altar

Leave all your doubts behind
I am a paramour of a special kind
My love never takes a day off
Satiety, subtlety, variety, anything you can think of

My love never takes a day off

LIFE AND DEATH

Each to his solitude in times like these
No scope for flocking like geese
Whatever happens in your aloneness
See you on the other side

If you take your last breath
Due to a heavy burden under your breast
Our times may be synchronized
See you on the other side

If you are destined to reincarnate
You are one of the fortunate
You will be pleasantly surprised
When I see you on the other side

If you are headed straight to the Father
And there's no place other
Do not be shocked to find me there
See you on the other side

If you are going to join the food chain
All the other options are in vain
I shall be there with you soon
See you on the other side

And if it so happens you survive
You sanitize, wear a mask, get sick, and be revived
I shall follow your exemplary lead
See you on the other side.

One world
One hope
One people
One destiny

Life and death

MY FRIEND

It is well with you my friend
Though we may differ in opinion
You will always be my friend till the end

It is well with you my friend
Diversity makes us strong
Makes us better anticipate a bend

You will always be my friend till the end
Though I know at times we are tempted
To unfairly judge and negative vibes to each other
send

It is well with you my friend
I will always respect your place in this world
In your absence your rights even defend

You will always be my friend till the end
My all weather comrade
Defending you from the proverbial fiend

Though, enmity, backstabbing, and hatred is the
trend
Rest assured I have your back and hope you have
mine
It is well with you my friend
You will always be my friend till the end

YOU, ME, MAYBE

52

You, me
Let's see
At crossroads
Cupid and Eros cross swords
We've tried
We've cried
Our chemistry weak
We don't speak
To each other
Like smitten lovers
You, me, maybe
I will call you babe
When the time comes
When we find love

WHO'S THAT GIRL?

How was he to know?
The demeanor didn't show
She was many people in one
Some cold, others fun

They rode waves of misery
Forgiving easily usually
But they did not understand
She was on a grandstand.

The many of her
He wished he knew her
Which one of her
Was or was not the real her

He suffered
She suffered
They suffered
Suffered suffered

Their children
Their kindred
Because he didn't know
Was he slow?

He came to realize
And to actualize
Fears causing tears
His dear was many dears.

It's rare
It's there
About one percent
Is she present?

KEEP YOUR OPINION AS OPEN AS THE GATES OF HEAVEN

Keep your opinion as open as the gates of heaven.
Remember there are nearly eight billion
experiences
The only correct position is that which has stood
the test of science
The opinions of our great-great parents were
proved wrong over time.

Remember there are eight billion experiences
It is a right to have an opinion
The opinions of our great-great parents were
proved wrong over time
The hallmark of a balanced person is an open mind.

It is a right to have an opinion
The only correct position is that which has stood
the test of science
The hallmark of a balanced person is an open mind.
Keep your opinions as open as the gates of heaven.

RHYMING IS NINE TENTH THE FLOW

Rhyming is nine tenth the flow
You do not have to rhyme at all
A poem catches a reader with rhyming I know.

A poem catches a reader with rhyming I know
Curious to find out how the rhymes go
And that improves the chance of a poem to glow

Rhyming is nine tenth the flow
Though some rhymes may be forced
The reader's interest, by the rhyme, is pulled in tow.

A poem catches a reader with rhyming I know
Some poets have problems with the left lobe of brain and so,
Instead of training it they hate rhyming for show.

Rhyming is nine tenth the flow
It is helpful to remember rhyming is aural
Know that no rhymes gnaw in prose

Let's not hate rhyming just because it's flawed.
It's one of the oldest poetic devices from nursery school.
A poem catches a reader with rhyming I know
Rhyming is nine tenth the flow

C. 210325

Deluke

Handsome, good

Dashing, ravishing, caring

Honest, dependable, trustworthy,   forthright

Manly, brotherly, fatherly

African, Negro

Muwanigwa

S.A.W.S

Winter (W) is reintroducing its classic modus
operandi
The chill you feel can kill
The lack of heat can stop the heartbeat
Air passages lined with slime, no time for the air to
repair its impaired lair
The chilly filly now comes with lethal asSASsins
assisting to ferret the life out of you
Summer(S) never hammers like a drummer with
invisible spikes
Autumn (A) automatically adjusts humidity with
humility for humans to ventilate very well
Spring(S) is the thing that brings natural herbs to
hedge against the invisible hegemony

Only Winter comes with the eerie illy contagion
with cold nonchalance, tipping the balance in
favour of death.
I swear I will wear warm apparel and task a mask to
scare the impertinent pestilence.
Summer Autumn Winter Spring
S.A.W.S
Minus the Winter is the S.A.S
Without the asSASsins.

UNKNOWN TIME TO AN UNKNOWN DESTINATION

Unknown time to an unknown destination.
We hurtle every day towards the finish line
No one knows when that line will appear on the
horizon
Our burdens we carry to the end.

We hurtle every day towards the finish line
Competing fairly sometimes, unfairly other times
Our burdens we carry to the end.
Some pretend to be in control of their fate to gain
advantage.

Competing fairly sometimes, unfairly other times
No one knows when that line will appear on the
horizon
But, some pretend to be in control of their fate to
gain advantage
To an unknown time and an unknown destination.

THE LAST DAY

Friday 31st December twenty twenty
What an ominous reflection.
31 reflects to 13
Hopefully Friday the 31st will not be like Friday the
13th
The signs have not been encouraging
Covid 19 uptrending
Cyclone Chalene upending
Friday
Might be the cry day
The last day
For many the last say

When the clock strikes midnight
I shall celebrate in hindsight
The new dawn
I will be on the phone
To one and all
Assuming I don't fall
On the terminal Friday
It won't be my trial day
The day I go to purgatory
For many, it's been mandatory
I wish all a safe last Friday
For December twenty-twenty the last day

STREET POETRY...DEVIL IN THE DARK

The night of Thursday, December Thirty twenty
twenty
My wife in the passenger seat talking plenty plenty
My brother's daughter in the back seat she too a
chatterbox
We had just bought takeaway food in a red box

At the flyover slowed down to traffic
When my BMW 525 was briefly static
A horrible explosive sound
My niece screamed I turned my head around

Passenger window shattered
Glass all over splattered
Niece cell phone gone
Nothing to do but drive home

The devil in the dark
With broken window I am stuck
My niece a nervous wreck
Just because I hit the brakes.

The ⬚ devil in the dark
Devil in the dark

FAR FAR AWAY

I am standing at the shore
Realizing more and more
That I am at the interface
At the coal face
So to speak
Anticipation at its peak

Behind me are fifty-six years of bruises
A litany of defunct truisms
None of them truthful
None of them fruitful
Turns out it was a game
A lame game for the tame

My father told me to obey rules
Rules are not for fools, he'd croon
But now I feel real thrill here
Standing facing the unknown without fear.

Unlike Lot's wife
I've no urge to look back to my previous life
Doesn't matter what things the future brings
The cacophony of verbal abuses in my soul rings

I am going away
Far far away
To another country
A country of poetry.

HALLELUJAH

I am awake, I am awake, I am awake
I am alive, I am alive, I am alive
Thank God, Thank God, Thank God
Hallelujah, Hallelujah, Hallelujah

Twenty-twenty is finally gone
Twenty twenty-one finally home
I escaped the suture
I am looking to the future

I reminisce many times when things went wrong
How I had to remain strong
Diseases, the deceased ceasing to exist
Suddenly not knowing they were at life's exit.

Another year
Another yeah
Another dance
Another chance

Hallelujah, Hallelujah, Hallelujah
Thank God, Thank God, Thank God
I am awake, I am awake, I am awake
I am alive, I am alive, I am alive

POEMYELITIS?

Everything I touch turns into a poem
That's a good thing
Right?
Like spontaneous combustion
It just happens

In my sleep
When I weep
In the bush
In the house

That's a good thing
Right?
After a fight
In darkness or light

In sadness
In happiness
That's a good thing
Right?

Don't know what this is
Perhaps a disease?
Poemyelitis?
Poemyelitis

LIFE IS.....

Life is so precious
A bubble by a bubble maker
You blink
It's gone
Torn
Flown
Gone like the wind
Gone indeed

Inside the bubble
A bundle
Dreams and hopes
An imaginary hoax
But it's real
You feel
Joy and pain
An insane train

Life is so so precious
Love it
Enjoy it
Give it
It's short
Give it a good shot
Live it

Then leave it

This life
Sometimes nice
The strife
The knife
May strike
You don't like
You die
That's life

WAIT AND SEE

I shan't be having any fear
Causing me to drink beer
dropping a tear
things are now clear

It's a new year
with a new yeah
a new way
I am a new man

Out with the old
all I have been told
lies so cold
so odd

I shan't prevaricate
to truth dedicate
even dictate
and indicate

My new year resolutions
a revolution
bringing solutions
to my evolution

I shall be my own man free
A new me
On the side of justice, I shall be
You wait and see

Wait and see

NATURE DOESN'T CARE

You can shout your opinion
Adverts on billboards you pin on
You can wrap yourself in philosophy
Verbosity without apostrophe
Nature is always there
Nature doesn't care

The adage of the ages
Written by sages in pages
Nature nurtures
Nurture nature
For nature to nurture you
This remains true

We have a global crisis
Worse than fundamentalist ISIS
Sanitize, wear a mask, social distance
Do that in this instance
To survive
It's costly to die and to revive

Those with strong opinions
About the cause and dominions
This is not the time
We will listen when things are fine
Though this problem is rare
Nature doesn't care

NATURE NEVER FAILS

73

It is not true
That............
And that...
Not true

It is true
This ....
And this.....
It's true

The question
Do you believe?
Should you?
Must you?

Choice is yours
If unsure
Trust nature
Nature never fails

SURPRISE SURPRISE

You never bother me
I bother you
You never make mistakes
I do the wrong things
You never apologize
I do the mea culpa

You never love me
I do all the loving
You never write me
I do the writing
You never phone me
I do the phoning

Surprise surprise
Now you beg me to stay
I stay not another day
Since you don't do
This time I won't too
Don't leave, stay, or whatever
I'm doing the leaving

STREET POETRY...REPLACING DOOR GLASS

The drinkers

It was my lucky day
This I have to say
First finding a replacement glass
For my BMW525 in its class
To find a place open a day before level three
lockdown
A place at Gaza land Shopping Centre, not town.
As of five January twenty twenty-one we are
shutting down
For one month the new strain of Covid 19 here in
town

I don't understand our leaders
Those who lead us
We were doing fairly well having lost about three
hundred
Our countrymen; our kindred
The new strain came to South Africa from the UK
Holidays upon us the border was opened assuming
it was ok.
A day or so the sick increased, casualties
rebounded

Lockdown level three mounted

I was so happy to find a glass and the fitters
I bought all the ten workmen a drink each; the
drinkers

IN LOVE WITH YOU

When I wake up
Before I even think of a teacup
When my brain gets into first gear
Before my brain remembers my fears
When I scan my body of pressures
Before I rush off for nature's censures
And prepare to face the new day
This is what I want to say

My first thought is of you
My last thoughts were of you
My dreams are about you
My daylight hours thinking of you

You you you you
The feeling is new
I'm in love with you
You you you you

MAKING SENSE OF THE SENSELESS

No, not again, will I take things for granted
This, our mother earth can get really upset dishing
us not what we wanted
All my life I have known things do change
I have experienced and witnessed many things
strange
This time the book of records will not have enough
pages
To keep an accurate record of all the happenings at
all stages
Nay, even cameras will not have enough memory
to capture every moment of this chimera.

The sun, our primary energy source, burps and
sneers at us causing erratic weather
Even our erstwhile friendly moon hides its visage
behind toxic cumulus clouds whose accumulated
toxins rain pain
Our only mother, the earth, seems to have
abandoned us the children she bore and swore to
nurture no matter this and that or what.
The air we breathe...we gasp ...the air is
impregnated with invisible particles bent on
depopulating all, the tall the short, all for the pall

I wonder, though, what shenanigan we have
wrought upon ourselves

I stand there, hand washing, clad in balaclava like a
militant, shunning every soul, trying to make sense
of it all.

Making sense of the senseless.

COMFORT ZONES

"The difficult and the easy incline towards each
other"

Philosopher spoke
Life is no joke
When the dust rises to cloud things
We hide behind artificial screens.
Hoping the problem goes away
Only to have it linger and stay

Problems have to be solved
All issues resolved
The difficult, the easy
Instead of being queasy
Postponing the agony
The truth and it's irony

Hiding in illusory homes
Our comfort zones.
Imaginary homes
Comfort zones

C. 210103

WOULD YOU...IF I GAVE YOU MY HEART?

If I gave you my heart
Would you ensure its fit
Seventy-two times it beats
Sluggish, you kiss to start

Would you care for it like your own
Plugging it's every leak
Keeping it pumping at peak
Would you be a permanent home

Would you take it for a walk
Fondling it when it's cold
Never letting sadness be told
Allowing it to freely talk

When it came to Auntie Mercy
Would you be free and not hide it
That this my heart is the only one fit
To grace your feminine intimacy

Yeah, if I gave you my heart
Would you never tear it apart
Would you...if I gave you my heart
If I gave you my heart.

TIME WILL TELL

82

Three cheers for this world
Incomparable to yore
Some planned to take over the world
Stacked up arsenals of conquest
Preached racial purity
Only to wither in obscurity

Some things never change
Evil lives on
God watches in horror
As secret societies emerge
Plan to usurp His power
And singe his flowers

Time will tell
Time will tell

THIS THING CALLED KISSING

This thing called kissing
So easy you can do it with your eyes closed
The build-up to a first kiss is a unique experience
You can also do it with eyes open.

So easy you can do it with your eyes closed
It causes your heartbeat to increase in anticipation
You can also do it with eyes open.
If you are a first-timer closing your eyes is
instinctive.

It causes your heartbeat to increase in anticipation
The build-up to a first kiss is a unique experience.
If you are a first-timer closing your eyes is
instinctive.
This thing called kissing.

THE EMOTION OF A REAL MAN

The emotion of a real man
Runs in me when I think of you
The emotion of a real woman
I hope runs in you when you think of me

Runs in me when I think of you
This deep affection for you
I hope runs in you when you think of me
I have no doubt I have found a home in you.

This deep affection for you.
The emotion for a real woman.
I have no doubt I have found a home in you
And the emotion of a real man.

I PROMISE

85

I can't promise you the sky
That would be a lie
Can't promise the earth
Or, to raise you upon death

Yes, I will be fond
I will buy a diamond
I will be truthful
I will be faithful

What I promise is this
I promise everyday a kiss
I shall love you every day
Love you in every way.

NEVER AGAIN

Father!
Where are you?
I went to the place I should find you
You were not there
People called your Name
Looking up at the ceiling
Raising hands in the air
Filled room with incantation

People with hearts of stone
Dressed in thorns
Breeding greed
Clothed in sloth
Full of prejudice
Injustice!
Hating
And stating it

Father!
I shan't be going there again
I won't
Never again.

I WROTE A BALLAD

I played songs for you on my acoustic guitar
Even tried going exotic on the sitar
Trying to put your love in tune
Even tried the good old lute

Not one to be discouraged
Not easily disparaged
I played upon a harp
Hoping a waltz would you disarm

The keyboard
Made you really bored
The sax
Made you relax

They made you sleep
No matter how deep
The note
Then I wrote

I wrote a ballad
Recited it aloud
Now my bed is your bed
My head next to your head.

WHEN YOU SAID YES! YES! YES!

Hippos yawned with disinterest
Not the slightest interest
Killers my foot!
Like they understood what was afoot
Crocs basking on the riverbank
But, I wasn't afraid, to be frank

I was afraid of what you'd say
On that day.
When the question I popped
When I proposed
You and I in a canoe
"Can love me, can you?"

When you said yes! yes! yes!
I felt totally blessed

C. 210120

I WANT IT

It cannot be adjourned
The judgement
If you don't love me
Set me free
No bail
Beyond the pale

Quid pro quo
There's got to be something
Specific performance
Romance
With me the fella
No contumelia

Vice Majeure
No excuse per se
Ignorance of the law no excuse
Love
Sine qua non
Bring it on

I need it
I feel it
Grant it
I want it

I SHALL, I WILL

Where you go I shall go
Where you sleep I shall lay my head
Where you live I shall live
When you cry I shall comfort you

Because I love you.
I love you
Whatever it is I shall, I will
Pass me any bill, I shall, I will

When you go down I go down with you
When you are ill I shall nurse you
When you are hungry I shall feed you
When you need love I shall love you

Because I love you.
I love you
Whatever it is I shall, I will
Pass me any bill, I shall, I will

THEY KNEEL TO PRAY

Some people live dead
In their chest a heart of lead
They watch a ship capsize
With the dead fantasize

(Hacking with machetes)
(Playing with matches)

They feel the thrill
Abet the kill
Watch a ship
Expose its keel

The living dead
Hearts of lead
See violence
Watch in silence

(The scism)
(Shhhhh!!!!)

Every week one day
They kneel to pray
For whom?
To who?

NAKED LIES

You said it
Your words fit
the narrative
But it's relative
The time will come
A girl in love
In birthday suit
For ruth
She tries
Naked lies

In that state
Will look at your face
No mask
And ask
"Do you love me?"
You'd be free
To stutter
Or stammer
But, in your eyes
Naked lies

"READ THE CLICHÉ"

If I came to you
We won't be understood
If you came here
I would've to be near
To explain to the curious
And say to the furious

"Read the cliché"
"On my t-shirt"
"Love is blind"
"Please be kind"

If we met in solitude
That would be so rude
Love should be in the open
Showing off, kissing often
Lost in time and space
Saying in every place

"Love is blind"
"Please be kind"
"Read the cliché"
"On my t-shirt"

MY BRAIN TELLS ME THIS, MY HEART THAT, MY SOUL THE ARBITER

My brain tells me this, my heart that, my soul the
arbiter
My soul takes over when my heart, the shrew,
argues with its crew, my brain
Oft times my heart wants despite the risk, my brain
counsels caution
Disagreements vicious, I end up in depression, my
heart in tantrum.

My soul takes over when my heart, the shrew,
argues with its crew, my brain.
I meditate in conversation with my soul, the arbiter
Disagreements vicious, I end up in depression, my
heart in tantrum.
My soul asks, "Would you wish it upon yourself";
the issue is settled.

I meditate in conversation with my soul, the
arbiter.
Oft times my heart wants, despite the risk, my
brain counsels caution.
My soul asks, "Would you wish it upon yourself";
the issue is settled.
My brain tells me this, my heart that, my soul the
arbiter.

SOUND LOVE

Receivers may be deceivers
A transceiver delivers, we thought
Even with waveguides
They wished our love died
Attenuated
They attempted
But, as lovers, we tried
Sighed and cried

We did the sound spectrum
Even hurting eardrums
Through the bandwidth
Full analysis done
Of the resonance
Of our romance
Our love
Sound love

What would we gain?
Straining our ears?
Worrying about interference,
Signals without reference
Poor in communication
Good at causing commotion
In our love

Our sound love

You and I are on the same wavelength
Having been at it at length
We brook no hacking
Or blocking
Of the transmission
And transitions
In our love
Sound love

WORDS

His father used words
Words that added a decade to the boy's age
At eight he was eighteen on his father's rage range
Words out of this world
WORDS!

Words part of a paternal arsenal
Words a pestilence with a mouth of its own
Words from lips trilling in fatherly recusal
Words propelled by inebriated vocal cords
Words with hardness
Words with harshness

The boy's spirits never broke
He never spoke about the WORDS
Wrote WORDS in prose
WORDS in poetry
Words out of this world
WORDS

RETREAT TREATY

I thought you were having fun
In bed and in the sun
Now I sit on the bench in the park
You left a permanent mark
On the bench
And In my bed

Was it a dream?
In the park eating cream
In bed doing stuff
Rough enough
Sharing our lives
Alive

Now you are gone
I mourn
I ask why
You left me high and dry
No goodbye
Why?

Even in war they do treaties
Peace treaties
Armistices
Detente
I'm waiting out in the street
For your retreat treaty

SOUL SEARCHING

I am looking for my soul
On my anatomy, I can't find it
Not in my brain
Nor in my heart
Not even in my gut

Perhaps if I could turn my eyes
in their sockets and look inside
If I could I would
But I doubt I would find it.
They keep telling me to look inside my soul

Is it a collection of memories etched on my mind?
Is it resident in the synapsis in my brain?

They say some people have no soul
No mercy
No compunction
They take life
With a knife
Or a gun
For them it's fun.

I don't do such
Not that much
But I still can't find my soul
Not at all

WE TRIP WHICHEVER WAY

We wake up
To trip into a new day
Drink tea in a cup
Maybe a tot of whiskey
A new day is wispy
No matter our daily plan
We play it's tune

To trip into a new day
We play its tune
A tune of sorrow
Tune of happiness
Tune of despair
Tune of hope
We Trip whichever way

SOME.......

Somehow there is life within death
That's how things rebirth themselves

Somewhere on this earth, there is death happening
A living thing succumbing to the excesses of nature

Someone is losing consciousness for the last time
Leaving behind whatever it was they held dear.

Something is replacing that which has expired even
as I write this.
The sea becoming land, land flooding with water

Somewhat, there are things we take for granted
because our lives are short
Even the sun, the earth, and the moon will renew
their ending.

Someday, somehow, everything will come to an
end due to something from somewhere.

HAVING FUN, HAVING PUN

He who hath no rhyme commits a crime
Fundies say rhyming kills the vibe
Disdain for matching sounds
Refrain is without grounds
Some make it a religion
Come to hate rhymes in all regions
At the start
Or end of the art
Poem rhymes
There are cries
Doesn't rhyme it's good
Easily understood
It's really easily just a reaction
To an action.
Left lobe of the brain rebelling
Sound patterns repelling

Let's start a rebel movement
To cause improvement
In the attitude
And Latitude
To which rhyming is accepted
Not excepted
And recite our motto
For our mojo

Let us rhyme
Make us smile
The simplicity
Multiplicity
Duplicity
Audacity
Of rhyme
That time
Makes us young again
Something to gain
Like little kids
Satisfy the need
Pranking
Skanking
Having fun
Having pun

WAKING UP TO THE UNKNOWN

Times have changed
I used to wake up to a pre-planned day
Now I wake up to the unknown.
Nothing surprises me anymore

It could be;
"The neighbour died last night"
The guy I last saw midnight
Full of life
Going on about what he disliked.

It could be; "There is no more work"
There is a shutdown due to a virus
Or the government has changed
Overnight
I just shrug my shoulders and think "Oh well",
that's alright.

There's something constant though,
The love of God is something I know.
Come rain come shine
I know with God's love I'll be fine

I'M STAYING

I'm staying
I'm no longer straying
No longer straying
I'm staying.

I wanted to escape
To the southernmost cape
Woke up in the dead of the night
To cross the border before light.

The car I wanted to use
To start it refuse
Two tyres flat
But not only that

I tried to fly away
On that fateful day
Passport was expired
Felt really tired

Tried going on foot.
Suitcase full of suits
Weighed me down
Could only frown

What was I thinking?
Forgetting my vows without blinking?
"In sickness and in health"
Not to ever depart in stealth.

WHEN I PART MY LIPS TO TALK TO YOU

When I part my lips to talk to you
It's like I raise the dead
You hate me instead
Talking is an understatement
You don't understand what's meant
Or is it you don't care
My welfare
It's warfare

It can't be right
When we fight
I write
You don't read
You don't see the need
I try to explain in person
When I part my lips to talk to you
It's like a declaration of war
You hate me the more

Let's do the needful
Though dreadful
You go your way
Here I will stay

Lick my wounds
Lick my lips
So there's no lisp
When I part my lips to talk to you
And say goodbye

ACROSTIC CAUSTIC POEM

A-bove our need to be heard
C-omes the need to be read
R-eading is a conduit for attention
O-ver ambient noise in detention
S-omeone can peruse a piece
T-ranslate the reading in peace
I-n their condition decide to do
C-urious things with the book
C-alling all prisoners to be patient
A-nd avoid becoming patients
U-nchained but still not free
S-uffering in a prison pit
T-ortured for insurrection
I-nstead of reading instructions
C-orrecting acrostic caustic POEM

RE-WRITE

Prison Time

P-eople justifiably hate prison time
R-egret the commission of a crime
I-n fact this is why states imprison
S-o offender can reflect on reason
O-ne should never be there
N-ot all throw their hands in the air
T-ime can be used to write
I-nstead of regretting your plight
M-any have earned degrees
E-ducating themselves for free

WHEN I.....I.

When I sit under a tree
I set my mind free
Write a verse of what I see
Writing pad on my knee

When I sit on a park bench
A bin throws quite a stench
I ignore, write a poem in French
French dictionary improving the extent

When I sit at the table
I am really comfortable
Discuss a poetic fable
Ideas making me able

When I go to bed I dream
Quite a poetry stream
Some making me scream
I never run out of poetry steam

BLESSINGS

Fluttering knots in my belly
Butterflies all sizes inside
Subzero water molecules in my spine

Upper palate a parched desert
Matrix of taste buds
Nothing to taste

Eyes out of focus
Rejecting their locus.
Bagged eyelids

A nervous twitch
A seismic occurrence
Going down the bend

A crippled man goes past
Legs blew off in war
Now i know
I have blessings

IN MY LIFE

When your lips parted
I knew from the start
In my heart
We'll never part

I fell
In a spell
Could tell
It was well

You spoke
A stroke
Holy smoke
I woke

A new life
Was nice
I was like
That's a wife

With a rose
I rose
To propose
In prose

To say
Come stay
Today
Everyday

You're nice
Be my wife
The wife
In my life

SOCIETY EXPECTS

Lonely I feel only when you are here with me.
When you are gone, gone is my one and only
moment of feigning affection.
I feel nothing in my void of nothingness, having
loved myself first alone.

Ostensibly, you came to occupy my sane senses
with intangible feelings of affection. A fiat only
existing through repetition and repertoire. You say
"I love you" so many times that I now believe I love
you too. But, I feel satiety in solitude. My alone
moments the best lonely moments without your
comments.

So, now, therefore, I say to you,
every time you tell me you love me, I say I love you
too because society expects it. So, ok, ok, I love you
too.

SO DEEP, FOR KEEPS

In my mind are several compartments
Dedicated to my commitment
To you, for you

Right compartment is full
Things I need to get for you
To make you happy, make you peppy

The left side is for memories of you
Good times we spent together
In the park, in the dark

The top section is for the future
Things I want to do with you
Our kids, our needs

The bottom is bottomless
Where I keep my love for you
So deep, for keeps.

CROSS

When I am cross I do the crossword puzzle.
I come across as a benign ass wearing a muzzle
My mind crisscrosses to the realm of life and death
The Cross, the Crucifix
Across, my tormentor sits arms crossed, gleefully
grinning.

Mr. Cross keeps harping on about the future
looking bright.
He makes me really cross with his selfishness.
While he lives large I eat promises and cross buns.
A mercenary with crossbones emblazoned on his
soul.

One day I shall become so cross with Mr. Cross I
shall pull hard on the crossbow and escape across
the oceans. Cross my heart.

MY WORD

If I die
Don't cry
When I die
Don't lie
How I die
Don' ask why
Time I die
Don't sigh
Why I die
Don't pry

Am here
No fear
Of death
On earth
I die
I try
To renew
Anew
My word
In world

My work
My word
Will live

Will give
The world
My worth
Alive
Alike
Or dead
Instead.

JUST LOVE?

Is it magnetism?
Whatever it is
I am hooked

I think of you
Want you
Only you

The path you take
I stray by mistake
For you

The bed you sleep
I'd sleep deep
With you

Food you eat
Best treat
For you

What is this?
Magnetism?
Or just love?

A REBEL WITH A CAUSE REBELLING FOR NO REASON

We the people who occupy this world
Sometimes we are cruel to each other
We create an unnecessary rebel
A rebel with a cause rebelling for no reason

Sometimes we are cruel to each other
We are supposed to hear no evil, see no evil, but
evil begets a rebel
A rebel with a cause rebelling for no reason
Will take up the cause even without a good reason

We are supposed to hear no evil, see no evil, but
evil begets a rebel
We create an unnecessary rebel
Who will take up the cause even without a good
reason.
We the people who occupy this world

BACK TO MY ROOTS

Poetry is self-expression
Whereas some want to give a different impression
It is best to be spontaneous
To achieve something momentous I used to write
well
Now i am on a dry spell
Reading too many styles
Bringing smiles
But scattering my art
To doubt myself I start

It is good to read other works
To measure your worth
But experiences are different Command of
language different Personalities different
Differences different

I have to go back to my roots
Wear my original poetic boots
And write and write and write
Even when they say my poems are not right.
I will let my poems take flight
Write what I want into the night.

"Way back from Goeffrey Chaucer, there had been much change in style form and everything. There is Victorian poetry, romantic poetry, modernist poetry, etc...even in sonnets, there is Petrarchan sonnet and Shakespearean sonnet..with a difference. There are many poetries that cannot be put in any of forms, but still, they exist...do just enjoy your poetic style and vibe.

But you say you just write poetry. It has nothing to do with self-expression..."

BECAUSE I LOVE YOU

Every second of every minute of, every hour of
every day.

Every week of every month of every year of every
decade.

Everything, every move, every, decision. every
action,

It has been and will always be about you and you
only.

Only you,
Because I love you

THE LONGEST MINUTE IN THE WORLD

After years of cultivating
Going forth to sow the seed
Supplying all the needs
Meticulous weeding
Feeding

You finally dropped the shocker
Said you only had a minute
My heart was torn apart, I mean it
You said this was the end
No longer my friend

In one minute you left
The shortest meeting
Fleeting
I still live that sixty seconds of horror
The longest minute in the world.

LOVE TIMETABLE

Since I was born
Spent years on my own
No one to phone to love
No one home to come
To have to hold or scold
Blankets I d fold when cold

Till we met at the table
I was able
To have my life stable
And a love timetable

You are my hon
Twice in the morn
Thrice I phone
Get your favourite corn
My love you've won
Had dinner for one

Till we met at the table
I was able
To have my life stable
And a love timetable

HUMAN RELATIONSHIPS MAY BE LIKE THAT

The so-called evil person may be the one who is
good
The most intolerant may be the person who
preaches tolerance
The one they label bad may be the most loving
person.
Human relationships may be like that.

The most intolerant may be the person who
preaches tolerance,
Stands in front pontificating with a forked tongue
Human relationships may be like that.
It is foolish to allow another mortal to control your
soul,

Stands in front pontificating with a forked tongue
The one they label bad may be the most loving
person
It is foolish to allow another mortal to control your
soul
The so-called evil person may be the one who is
good

THAT'S ME

My life, my time, my sign, my instance in the
distance
I began, I swam, with a bang, I sang
I am new, like you, that's true, I can do without you
Hug me, tug me, bug me, shrug me
See me, free me, beat me, trick me, let me be
I live, I give, I forgive, I believe, that's me.
It took no fluke, rebuke the spook, the crook, in the
book
Lovers, my mother, my father, then brothers and
sisters, then me.

WRITE IT DOWN

My communications professor asked.
"Between the words kikiriki and oumbooloomboo
which one sounds male and which sounds female?"
It was unanimous that the former was male
The latter was female.
It did not matter what language you speak. This
was true universally.

There is verbal communication and non-verbal
communication.

What makes poetry wonderful is that we write our
thoughts down. We want to communicate
something. Non-verbal communication is not the
best way to communicate with a bard.

Write it down.

Subliminal messaging is understood, though rude,
it is non-verbal communication. Completely
unnecessary.

SOMETIMES IN ANGER, THERE IS TRUTH

Sometimes in anger there is truth
A person you thought was a friend
When you are not there behaves uncouth

He smiles when you are there, behind says you are
fool
Displays so much anger
Sometimes in anger there is truth

He is quick, about you, to speak untruth
Pretends he knows a lot more about you
When you are not there behaves uncouth

His patronizing jokes are crude
To bring your reputation to his level
Sometimes in anger there is truth

When you are in a bad mood
He sheds fake crocodile tears
When you are not there behaves uncouth

His morbid jealousy of you is understood
He works hard to display his anger
When you are not there behaves uncouth
Sometimes in anger there is truth.

MAY LITTLE ONES WARM YOUR HEART

Affection comes in small doses
Love from little children
Their innocence
Their purity of heart
When they look into your eyes
and say, "I love you, mommy"
Your heart melts
Pure love is felt
The stress of work goes away!
May little ones warm your heart.

A spouse who cares
Your significant other goes out of their way
Remembers your birthdays
Your favourite drink
And reminds you of their commitment to you
A little touch here
A peck on the cheek
Do unusual favours
Little ones
May little ones warm your heart

I CAN'T KEEP CALM BECAUSE YOU EXCITE ME

I can't keep calm because you excite me.
I try to pretend you are not there
I even walk and talk nonchalantly next to you
The truth is your effect on me is more than skin
deep.

I try to pretend you are not there
When you are close my skin itches with desire
The truth is your effect on me is more than skin
deep.
When you are not there I feel lovesick like seasick.

When you are close my skin itches with desire
I even walk and talk nonchalantly next to you
When you are not there I feel lovesick like seasick.
I can't keep calm because you excite me.

I GO THROUGH THE RUSTY SHELVES OF MY LIFE

I go through the rusty shelves of my life
Marvel in disgust at sad memories, but happy to be
alive
And wonder if any mortal has the right to tell me
what it's like

I have been to places dark and bright
I have stashed terabytes of rich memories
And wonder if any mortal has the right to tell me
what it's like

I go through the rusty shelves of my life
Out of love for humanity, I share my experiences
Only to have shallow-minded people turning my
day to night

I wonder if any mortal has the right to tell me what
it's like
To be who I am, what I am, and what I want to be
If you cannot look honesty in the face get a knife

Stick it up and down your soul and twist it right

It does not matter what you believe, it matters only
what you do
I go through the rusty shelves of my life

And write poems and stories of my life late into the
night
Are you sure you can wear my shoes, my soul, and
my skin?
I go through the rusty shelves of my life
And wonder if any mortal has a right to tell me
what it's like.

SOMETIMES I AM UP, SOMETIMES I AM DOWN

Sometimes I am up, sometimes I am down.
I feel like a captain less ship on a choppy sea
One second a rush of euphoria the next
shipwrecked
I feel like curling into a ball in a tortoiseshell.

I feel like a captain less ship on a choppy sea
I crave your strong arms to guide me.
I feel like curling into a ball in a tortoise shell
Only you can save me with open arms.

I crave your strong arms to guide me.
One second a rush of euphoria the next
shipwrecked.
Only you can save me with open arms.
because sometimes I am up, sometimes I am down.

THE MIND

T-he mind
H-er bind
E-very thought behind
M-ood unkind
I-n it you find
N-othing refined
D-amn the mindset

BRIDGE TO RIVERSDALE FARM

It stands there a stoic
Steadfast, heroic
Many souls carried
The singles, the married
The dead
The dread
Sometimes submerged
Floodwaters from streams all merged

The bridge to Riversdale Farm
Never does any harm
Taken for granted
Like it's not wanted
One day when she is gone
We gonna be cut off all alone

ABOUT THE AUTHOR

DELUKE MUWANIGWA

I was born on June 18, 1964 in southern Zimbabwe, in a village called Chivi, in Masvingo Province. At the time, Zimbabwe was under Ian Smith's government and a guerrilla war was in its infancy to free the country from colonial rule. I have scant memories of my early days, but the difficult rural life and occasional abuses I went through, stir sad memories in me sometimes. Some of it is captured in my poems.

In 1973 I moved to Zambia to escape the escalating bush war. In December 1977 my father inexplicably decided to immigrate back to the then

Rhodesia at the height of the war and his nationalist activism eventually took his life in August 1979.

On April 18, 1980, Zimbabwe got its Independence from Britain. At that point, I went back to school to repeat my grade seven, passed, and went to Lord Malvern High School, in Waterfalls, a suburb of Harare, where I met my wife. Our affair started when we were in form two in 1982, she being 15 years old and I, being 18 years old.

We were in the same class for the 6 years of our secondary school, passed well, and went to the University of Zimbabwe. I studied electrical engineering and she studied pharmacy.

We are still together today, nearly 40 years later. We have two children, Dananayi and Mudiwa Nathasia.

The question on many peoples' minds may be; what's an electrical engineer doing writing poetry?. Beats me, but, it's something I have a natural passion for. I did not go to poetry school, though I wish I had, and I have learned poetry the hard way; through reading poetry and interacting with other poets on poetry fora. Enough said. Enjoy the poems.